REAL ESTATE

HOBBY

MILLIONAIRE

By Bonnie Laslo

DISCLAIMER AND/OR LEGAL NOTICES

Contents

Develop your new *profitable* hobby after work...

Don't be a landlord!

Get started in real estate investing in 30 minutes!

IT'S STILL REAL ESTATE!

Stupidly Simple

The **SECRET** Golden Key *everyone* has been asking for........ you can be a

Quick Millionaire

much *faster* with a

Billionaire Team

"Time is valuable. Teams are best.
Use them both wisely and I will show you success."

\- Bonnie Laslo

Allow me to shave off *years*
to your success time.

Is This Worth Reading?

I am 31 years young... I hit my first goal of
$1,000,000 in real estate at the age of 26.

So, *yes*, it's worth the read.

You'll grow as a person!

Model my actions to get my results.

I can do it, you can do it...because I'm *STILL* doing it;
come on, it's a no-brainer.

Don't believe me?

Well, come join my team and you can experience it in
real time.

Don't take my word for it. Come and see for yourself!

Do it with hands-on training going through a rental
property real estate transaction, up front and center,
if you like.

WARNING

I have written this book as a

HOW-TO INSTRUCTION MANUAL

Follow the directions to success.

SIMPLE + SIMPLE = MASSIVE SUCCESS

Reference Steps 1-5

You DO NOT have to read the entire book to get started. **Get started <u>now</u>** *with STEP #1, then move on to the other four steps, and you can have rental property cash flowing from your new HOBBY.*

Then nothing new...you just...

* * * * *

COMPLETE & REPEAT

* * * * *

Over and over and over and over again!

Get a couple, or a few, rentals to cover your own mortgage or run with it to Millionaire status.

FREEDOM. It's *your* choice.

In this book you will get an overview...

Of all the important information from the real estate
and business millionaire books I've read, plus
all the seminars and mentors that I have gained great
knowledge from—it's all here.

But I'll save you from all the 'fluff.'

I still highly suggest you learn from these people and
others you encounter.

Each time you will grow as a person.

Education was, and still is, the key for me.

But it STILL could have been *much* simpler.

That is my purpose for this book:
to make things simpler for *you*. The book is also my gift to
the people whose lives will be changed. It is the simple
realization of the freedom real estate investing provides.

Notice and think about this:

Most of the Rich, and definitely the Wealthy, have a relationship with...guess what?

Yes, Real Estate Investing!

The Best Game of
Follow-the-Leader
I have ever played.

94% of wealth in the US is from REAL ESTATE.

Don't try and reinvent;
absorb this knowledge.

I keep it simple!

I make it fast!

I will tell you *exactly* what *you* can do & what I *did!*

FOREWORD

By Real Estate Billionaire
Ed Mercer, "Mr. Costa Rica"

The Real Estate Hobby Millionaire steps have the foundation all interested real estate seekers should read, and use to help the world become a better place.

The business style of cooperative business is a win-win situation that we can all model. They are stepping stones for all those new and experienced to follow toward the goal of success.

Success is both in business and in the improvement of those people around you. Use this as a guide and make a difference in your life.

FAMILY is one of the most important aspects to strive for, so have a wealth-building hobby with your friends and family just makes sense.

Ed Mercer

See You in Costa Rica

"You're already in Real Estate?
Then you know this is the *REAL DEAL!*"

Kimber Lim
LA Performance Magazine

Falicia Middleton

(Purchased 1ˢᵗ rental house through Hobby Millionaire course)

I just wanted to say *thank you* for all the help, advice, and time you put into helping me with my first real estate deal.

I have been looking for someone like you guys for about two-and-a-half years. I wanted someone who would help hold my hand through the entire process, from beginning to end. In my best interest my first deal, as we all know, didn't go according to plan. There were lots of road blocks and brick walls throughout the process and you were there by my side the whole time. Your one-on-one coaching and the conference calls helped tremendously in guiding me down the right path with each and every question and situation I had. Every time I got off a call with you, I would always say "I love them so much, they are so smart, I can't wait till I am where they are now." I also want to say that I appreciate the fact that you make sure that things are done when they need to be done and that you do things the right way. (No, short cuts.)

I learned so much more than I ever could have imagined on this first deal. I have grown stronger as a person and smarter as a RE investor, all because of you and Patrick. If I would not have had you by my side, I don't know if I would have made it to the end. Your advice and encouragement was vital in my success. With your one-on-one coaching program, I was able to successfully close on my first deal. I told you before, Bonnie, this is like a dream come true, and I really mean that!

- *Falicia Middleton*

Wendy Hatton

Hi Bonnie,

Thank you so much for your gift of time, enthusiasm, and knowledge that you made to the CEOSpace Central Florida group. It was a delight to hear you speak with such confidence and knowledge. You were an inspiration to everyone. all the guests at the preview meeting were impressed that someone with such obvious talents and achievement, a self-made multi-millionaire, would value CEOSpace so highly—and they saw the value for their business and their passion.

Thank you for taking the time to extend your vacation by a day to serve in the Club and for bringing some of your team. You deserve to do well as a platform speaker and author. This is only the beginning. You are a rising star. Let me know how we can serve you—it will be a pleasure.

Yours in gratitude,

Wendy Hatton
CEOSpace Central Florida

Susan Stewart

(Real Estate Investor & Property Management)

I want to take this opportunity to tell you how much I admire your ability to see the vision and then work toward it.

For years now, I've witnessed your determination and drive firsthand, and I love how you help others along the way.

Thanks for all you've done for me.

- Susan Stewart

Barbara Alviar

(Barbara inspires me in so many ways)

A very intelligent person.

A person who never turns her back on anyone. Very loving and always caring about other's feelings, or what they are thinking. Very outgoing and fun to be around. My counselor in good times or bad times. Most of all, a person that I can honestly say is a true friend. A person who does not give up on anything or anyone.

My Quote for the World:

"Always run to your goals,
because walking will only take longer."

- *Barbara Alviar*

Kevin Kolinski

(Jack-of-all-Trades & Business owner)

In my lifetime, I have rarely, if ever, encountered an individual who *successfully* combines warmth of heart with an incredibly high level of business acumen, like Bonnie Laslo.

In truth, her business success is powered as much by her love and kindness as it is by her strong will and determination to succeed.

> *- Kevin Kolinski*
> Six Six Media LLC

To quote the words of the Dalai Lama,

"When we feel love and kindness toward others, it not only makes others feel loved and cared for, but it also helps us to develop inner happiness and peace."

Steve Belding

(State Certified Real Estate Appraiser II, Real Estate Instructor, Real Estate Broker Instructor, & Real Estate Appraiser Instructor, etc.)

I highly and fully recommend Bonnie Laslo for any real estate-related needs you might have during the ongoing full and complete life cycle of property ownership and operations; namely, the buying, managing, and selling of any of the five classic property types: residential (especially multi-family), commercial, industrial, agricultural, and special-purpose/special-use properties.

- *Steve Belding*

Alex

(Who likes to fly under the radar, so I'll call him by his first name. this is the man who taught me how to play big. His support & guidance changed my life & the lives of thousands & thousands of people with his ripple effect...and the greatest part is he doesn't even know it...till now when he reads this book, "Thick & Thin." Alex)

Bonnie is one of the hardest-working people I know. She is a go-getter and does not know the word 'quit.'

I am very glad she is a partner of mine in many deals.

-   Alex

Patrick O'Donnell

(Rapid 0-100 Hobby Millionaire in the making)

Bonnie has been a fantastic mentor during the introduction phase to real estate investing.

She guides you on the correct type of property to purchase, and how to successfully manage it. She dedicates as much energy and effort to your success as she does her own.

It is her "never quit" mentality that is not only motivating, but also inspirational.

- *Patrick O'Donnell*

Queen Bonnie's Benchmarks

2 CRITERIA

Or we don't play.

On the next page is a portion of the coaching and training material I use in my real estate education program.

You should understand my level of dedication to people seeking to improve their lives and those of their families, too. It is difficult for me to watch people's lives circle the drain.

Excuses, complaints, blaming, and justifications don't exist in a true Hobby Millionaire's life.

It's sad and frustrating when you want more for other people than they want for themselves, plus it is a waste of a lot of time.

Thus the creation of:

THE COMMITMENT

Hobby Millionaire Coaching and Training Form

YOUR GOAL: Your commitment to me is to purchase at least five (5) rental units per year; otherwise, I must let you go from my training. Do what you have to do to get it done. There is absolutely NO reason for you to fail to accomplish your committed goal, unless your WHY isn't big enough. If I suspect this sooner, I reserve the right to discontinue training. I only work with serious Real Estate Investors.

Hobby Millionaire Trainee

Signature _____

STEP #1

GET
STARTED
NOW

Training #1

What TYPE of Rental Properties are for you?

Houses. Working class rentals that everyone can afford is highly recommended, although there are ways of making all types of properties work.

You will be taught how to make it work.

Depending upon what you can handle, the lower the purchase price of the property the better in my opinion:

Why?

You can buy more of them faster. Plus in the beginning, it is a more conservative amount to play with, until you learn how to play the game of real estate investing.

BUT, stay within your comfort level.

Hopefully, I can stretch your comfort level and get you to see houses in a totally different light, so ALL of the opportunities are available to you.

Exercise #1

If you do *not* own your own home, then that automatically becomes your first investment property.

Discuss or think of what type of house you can live in that's simple and affordable to start.

What are you currently paying in monthly rent? Is that monthly payment affordable for you?

Write down that number, and then multiply it by 100, or add 2 zeros to your number.

What do you get?

Example: $900/month = $90,000 purchase price.

This number will be in the price range you search for. If you plan on renting the rooms and having roommates, then you could work the numbers for a higher-priced house.

An important tip is: always base your number on *one* person's income. That way, if something unexpectedly ever happens, you won't lose your house. Unfortunately, many people find themselves in this position.

This is due to buying, where it takes both people to pay the mortgage. Under my training in this book, I will not teach you this method of purchasing. Hobby Millionaires are conservative and safe investors.

We enjoy low risk and large profits with an awesome future upside.

Exercise #2

Already own your home?

Congratulations!

Discuss what type of house you can see yourself renting to people.

Examples are fixer-uppers, turnkey, new construction, etc.

1. What type of people are your tenants?

2. How much monthly rent do the tenants pay?

3. Do they have pets?

4. Are they students? Seniors? Young professionals?

5. Is there an area around you in which you'd like to own rental houses?

6. What three areas?

Really think about this and determine a good starting point.

As you begin to get familiar with the process of investing, you will notice and work towards including all types of tenants where your two criteria can be found or created.

© 2008 **Bonnie Laslo**

For those people already familiar with real estate, please put aside all your past experiences that might conflict with the next process of evaluating the properties, please.

I can't tell you how many people, even to this day, tell me these criteria don't exist and that I don't know what I'm talking about, or that it is impossible.

If so...then how-in-the-world do a zillion other investors, including myself, have a multi-million-dollar portfolio full of them? And how are we still purchasing them?

Hmmmmm...

For the new investors where this is going to be your first rental property, just know ahead of time that you're going to hear these types of things.

No worries, because those people are probably broke working a job.

Spot them, love them for your differences in opinion, and move on to being rich like the other Hobby Millionaires. Each person chooses what path they take in life, you won't take that one.

If you're reading this book, then you know there is a better way. That's because you're smart. Of course there is!! You might even know me, or knew me back when I was in the grocery store with a calculator buying ramen noodles and raviolis. Haha! Yes, all too true.

Okay, here we go.

This is what you're going to do, and here are the two criteria broken down and explained in layman's terms:

HOW do you find your rental properties?

(Here are a few simple ways I find some of mine. Use these.)

1. Real Estate Agents: a good agent is worth the money. Ask for all listings within your price range. Under $100k per house, or under $50k per unit for apts. (We will go over the numbers in detail to figure out what that number is for you shortly).

2. Real Estate Ride: ride around with a family member or partner. This is easier because the other person can write down information, so you don't run into people. Ha-ha!

3. Online Opportunities: scout for houses online.

   - Various Realtor.com websites

   - MLS

   - Loop Net

   - Craigslist

   - Local newspapers

   - For Sale by Owner Sites

   - Etc.

There are other methods, but these are the ones we're going to focus on. Why? Because they work for finding your first property (or next one if you're already playing).

Some other, more advanced, examples:

* Lis Pendens lists – These are the lists of people who have been served with foreclosure papers. They are going to lose their house if they don't figure something out.

**Regarding Real Estate Agents, I suggest looking online at the types of properties you like, and see which listing agent is handling these types of properties. That will be the person you want to build a relationship with.

Reminder

Real Estate Agents are real estate agents for a reason. They like the art of selling, we like the art of investing. I don't wish to offend anyone who is an agent, but my experience is that a majority of them do not understand or favor your methods of investing. They like the simple system they were taught, but there are a TON of different ways to buy. Not just one.

Now remember always. You are an investor. You are the buyer. You play your game of investing however you feel like playing it, ALWAYS. That's why real estate is fun, you can do it your way.

Please understand that they may not be on the same level of understanding you are, unless they have rental properties themselves. This makes it a lot easier to explain.

Please don't listen to them without verifying information, because many can be new and still learning the process. Most are great at finding what you're looking for in their bucket of houses but there are other ways to buy houses. Although, again a great real estate agent is worth their weight in gold. When you find the agent who plays the real estate process your way, be sure to keep them and use them in all your deals. Even the ones you find on your own. Trust me, it will be beneficial to you in the long run. Both of you can help each other and make more profits faster.

So at this time, try thinking about this. The more you do this particular process, the easier it will be to see the deals. Eventually, they will pop out at you. I promise.

This is where your new hobby begins.

Exercise

Look on Craig's List (www.craigslist.com) for properties that fit the numbers.

Look in the Sunday newspaper for properties in your price range.

Online Opportunities – scout for houses online.

- Various Realtor.com websites

- MLS

- Loop Net

- Craig's list

- Local newspapers

- For Sale by Owner Sites

- Etc.

Eventually, you will call the Real Estate Agent about one online property you find; then go look at it in the up coming steps if it meets the Bonnie Benchmarks.

Reality Talk

So...Instead of sitting on the couch after work with snacks in your hand, watching other people's lives on TV or playing that video game for another five hours or taking random naps since you're bored or playing with your web page or reading that non-purposeful book to entertain yourself.

At least get out your lap top and have it in your lap while watching this lovely mindless numbing TV or take a break from it for an hour or two.

Eventually, you will choose to convert your non-productive or non-profitable hobbies into periods of leisure surfing of the internet, newspaper, etc. for properties.

Some of you also have kids that are constantly on the internet already (or significant others), so this can also be a valuable activity to teach your children (or your significant other). Let them know what you're looking for and chances are they can spin out a few in a matter of minutes.

Scouting for Your New Properties

(This is exactly how I do it.)

Here we go:

Do you know of any people selling a house?

If so, how much would it rent for?

Then, let's see if the numbers work for you.

Criteria #1
Scouting the $200 benchmark

The property *must* have a $200+ monthly NET profit.

This is your benchmark. We buy *NO* houses that don't have at least a $200 monthly profit.

THIS IS A PROMISE
YOU MUST KEEP *FOREVER!*
Got it?

These are Queen B'S benchmarks for fast-track assessment of properties:

$100,000 = $1,000/month rent to break even + $200 profit
= $1,200 is what it has to rent for.

$80,000 = $800/month rent to break even. + $200 profit
= $1,000 is what it has to rent for.

$50,000 = $500/month rent to break even. + $200 profit
= $700 is what it has to rent for.

Remember that you do <u>not</u> want to break even, you want to <u>make</u> money.

Note: you want $100-$200 net profit per unit for multi-family properties.

If you can't get that much, **walk away**...but at least make an offer of what the property is worth to you, based on your numbers.

Examples of how to get the #'s:

$100,000 House = $1,200/rent minimum rent to meet Criteria #1

$80,000 House = $1,000//monthly minimum rent

$50,000 House = $700 monthly minimum rent

$30,000 House = $500 monthly minimum rent

When you're looking at or calling on a rental property, this should be your first concern: it either needs to be currently rented at these rates or you need to be able to rent it for this amount. Already rented is always better!

How do you find out rents?

1. Newspaper.

2. Call other "For Rent" signs around that house.

3. Management Companies: call and ask.

4. Apartment Complex Managers.

5. Apartment Guides: these give you great benchmarks; although the house should rent for a bit more than an apartment.

6. Ask neighbors in the same neighborhood as the house.

7. Ask a person who is renting nearby.

8. Ask someone at the grocery store nearby.

9. Ask another investor or at investor groups.

10. Ask a student if you're in a student area.

Criteria #2
Understanding CAP rates

We buy at 9-10% or higher CAP rates going into the deal.

You should have this in place at closing or know 100% that you can rent it for the amount you based your numbers on.

Cap Rate = Annual Net operating income (NOI) / Purchase Price

Note: NOI is the annual forecasted NOI for the upcoming 12 months.

Example:

Gross monthly rent:		$ 1000
Expenses:	Taxes	($ 200)
	Insurance	($ 50)
	Maintenance	($ 100)
	Utilities	($ 0)
Monthly NET Operating Income		**$ 650**
Monthly $650 x 10 months -		**$6,500**

(the extra two months to round out the year are for 'oops' items).....just add a zero (0) to Operating Income

Property is worth at max $65,000 to you.

CAP = $ 6,500 / $65,000 = 10% CAP   Good Deal—PROCEED

Now, if this property is on the market for an asking price of $80,000, your offer should be at the price YOU need.

DO NOT start thinking about what the seller may or may not think. This is just an offer that works for you. And if it works for them, great!

Inflated asking or listing prices are normal, because they know the eventual selling price will be negotiated downward from the original asking price. So if they are asking for 80k, just offer them$54,600, it's lower than the $65,000 that is the max you can pay for the property.

Listen to Carlton Sheets' fantastic recommendation:

If you're not embarrassed about your offer, chances are you're offering way too much!

I understand this is going to feel very, very, very strange for some of you, but always know the seller can (and will) counter back on your offer with whatever they are comfortable with. Your uncomfortable feeling will pass— I promise you. The more offers you make, the faster you'll buy houses and get to your ultimate goal. Feel free to blame it on "your partner," but realize it is the price that works for us and fits in with our plans for the house.

A Seller will never do anything that's not right for them and their situation. Always, always, always remember this important concept.

STEP #2

LETTERS

OF INTENT

(LOIs)

Training #2
Your Status

You have found properties which have numbers that work.

- Minimum $200 per month NET profit (100-200+per unit for multi-family).

- At least 10% (preferably higher) Cap Rate going in to closing.

Letters of Intent (LOIs)

REMINDER: Inflated asking or listing prices are normal because the seller knows that the ultimate selling price will be negotiated down.

NOTE: Letters of Intent are a nightmare for most real estate agents. They will want you to sign their contract with one of your letter of intent options on it.

DO NOT do this unless you really feel you like the property and if you do, have the agent write up all three of your options into contracts and present those choices to the seller. Real Estate Agents will want you to do it their way to ensure they get paid a commission. Plus that's just what they have been taught. It's ok. You can also just add your LOI as an addendumn at the end of the contract. The addendumn in general means ...anything written on this paper wipes out anything in the contract above. So you can use their contract and add your Letter of Intent to the end of it.

The Letter of Intent doesn't have the wording for the commission agreement, so they sometimes get worried that you will be going around them if an introduction is made without their contract signed. You can attach your Letter of Intent to their contract as an addendum again to make all parties happy.

© 2008 **Bonnie Laslo**

Reminder again from Carlton Sheets (this is one of my favorites—remember this!):

"If you're not embarrassed by your offer, chances are you're offering way too much!"

Rules

1. Always use Odd Offers: $98,400 vs. $98,000; or $102,100 vs. $100,000.

2. Offer 3 to 5 options per LOI.

3. Give one offer to the RE Agent (if any) and mail one to the Owner/Seller.

4. Research online how much the seller paid and when, as well as whether they own other properties (use the official property appraiser website).

5. Make a file for each property; revisit it in 30 to 60 days if it's still on the market.

What's Your Offer?

How Much Should It Be?

What should be the offer and how much is the house worth to me?

Who cares what the seller is asking as a purchase price?

Not me... unless it's lower than what I'd offer.

1. What is it rented for? $1,200?

2. Minus my $200 Net Profit benchmark = $1,000.

3. Drop a zero...*Bam!* That's how much it's worth to you. $100K is your maximum offer.

Suggestions

Submit three options:

1. A FULL PRICE OFFER to buy, with the terms you like.

2. A CONVENTIONAL offer, which means you'll go to the bank to buy.

3. A Rent-to Own option, or even a Cash Option.

Don't worry; be happy. When the numbers work, any smart Real Estate investor will help with the cash part.

You always have to have the deal in hand, then the money shows up. It's pretty great how it works.

Remember to make the letter look simple, not *too* professional. You want to look like you're an average Joe or Jane.

Look non-threatening and kind of average, like you're looking to buy only your 2nd or 3rd rental house. We're looking for an air of simplicity, not complexity...you know, smart enough to buy but not successful enough to pay full price because you're semi-broke. You know their place can bring you some extra monthly income. You're just looking for a good solid investment opportunity or two.

Sample Letter of Intent
Use Your Numbers

Assume the house rents for $1000/month. The seller's asking price is $135k.

This means house is worth $80,000 at most, or a maximum payment on the house of $800 in order to fulfill the two criteria.

(ADDRESS HERE)

Hello,

I recently found your listing for the above house, and I would like to express my sincere interest in purchasing the property with one of the following options that would create a winning situation for all involved.

Option 1: Total Purchase Price of $135,000

- Monthly payments to you would be $800/month until the balance is paid off.

- Balloon payment in 60 months (sounds better than 5 years; a balloon is simply an *option* for you).

Option 2: Total Purchase Price of $84.300

- $500 down payment

- Seller installs new AC (or some other large-ticket item, because I don't really want you to pick this option. LOL)

- $4,300 credit at closing for each property. (notice how this brings it back down to $80k you need)

- Seller to provide survey (so you can save money and simply recertify it).

Option 3: Total Purchase Price of $141,000
(Yes, note the price is higher than the asking price.)

So the seller might really like this option and pick it.

- Payments of $800 on a rent-to-own, or lease option.

- Half of rents credited toward the purchase price.

- 60-month lease with option.

- Purchase in "As-Is" condition.

- Note: In this option the seller actually sells the property for more than the $141k. He also got the extra $400/month cashflow over the 60 months. Win-Win for both of you. With your $400 rent credit over that time period, you have a big credit at closing, too.

Option 4: Total Purchase Price of $47,300
(Yes, this is a no-brainer price if accepted; thus the cash will show up for you if you get this price.)

- Cash purchase.

- Bought in "AS-IS" condition.

Clear Marketable Title in all of the above sale scenarios

Thank you for taking the time to look over this multiple offer proposal. I look forward to hearing from you by 5:00 p.m. Eastern standard time, Wed., April 23, 2008. I'm leaving town soon, so time is of the essence.

Feel free to give me a call at (123) 456-7890 if you have any questions.

Sincerely,

Hobby Millionaire in the making

STEP #3

LOOK/INSPECT

&

LOCK-IN

the DEAL

Training #3

Your Status

An option on your LOI has been accepted:

- You will use an Inspection Sheet when you go out on site.

- Don't tell the Agent you are new because you're not going to consider yourself new. Remember, you have me, a successful, advanced Real Estate investor by your side who is mentoring you. You are modeling all the core important items to get that rental property and the life you want. Be confident, polite, and ask them the questions we go over in training. Make them your new Real Estate friend and contact because you can never have too many friends in your network.

Inspection & Locking in the Deal

REMINDER: If you don't feel comfortable doing your own inspections, feel free to hire a professional inspector, but I still want you to go out to the property. If you hire an inspector, meet them at the property and watch what they are doing. This will teach you and bring your attention to important factors to look for.

The inspector is there to find everything that's wrong with the house—large and small. Understand this is valuable as a negotiation tool. Some of the items will be important and some not. You will have to determine which items you can view as cosmetic verses the items that *really* keep the property from functioning as a rental property for you.

Tip to save money and be efficient... ask a maintenance person or a contractor to get the house ready for a tenant to move-in.

"Repair Quotes—meet your inspection needs...and meet a new contractor friend as well!"

- Bonnie Laslo

Instructions & Details

1. You've been contacted by the Seller, and the seller has selected one of the options you offered. The Seller wants to go to contract with the agreement.

2. Now, time to inspect the property. Always inspect before going to contract. Some contracts might not have an exit clause if something major is wrong with the property—you could *lose* your deposit money. It is a possibility, so *do not* place yourself into that situation. *Period.*

3. Dress casual like a contractor or a worker bee.

   Agents and sellers like working-class appearances during the inspection.

   - If they let you go alone, great!

   - If you're too youthful looking, take an older friend with you for credibility.

DO NOT: Show up dressed to the nines, in a Mercedes, with a big huge diamond ring on, or with an attitude of arrogance. Be nice and polite, but confident. There is a big difference between arrogant and confident—please notice the difference.

---

4. Show no emotion, be pleasant, and become friends with the agent or seller. The evaluation of the real estate deal is based on the numbers, *never* emotion. It either meets the two criteria or it does not.

   Don't show any excitement that you love the great deal or the house!

5. Follow an inspection sheet, line item by line item, until you're comfortable with it. Do a test on your own house to get in the flow of how to do it. Do this exercise with your spouse, kids, or friends! It's amazing what they see and what you do not see.

EXERCISE
to do with someone in your house

Do this exercise separately from each other.

Have one person do the outside inspection first and the other person do the inside inspection so you're in different places, then switch positions.

When you're both done, go over each other's inspection sheets.

---

6. Items to take with you: flashlight, tape measure, bug/flea spray, pen, inspection sheet, and a clipboard (I use the kind that lifts up to place items into it, remember the kind your high school gym teacher had all the time. It's perfect!)

7. On the first time getting out of the car to meet, *don't* pull the clip board/items out yet. Take a moment to meet, greet, and establish some rapport with the seller or agent.

8. **IMPORTANT:** open the window blinds and leave them open when you leave so you can begin sending people to the house to peek in. I have leased many houses prior to even owning them. (The agent might think you're doing this to see better in light.) Prospects who really like the home will give you a deposit and application before you even go to closing on it.

9. Now, go back to the car, pull out your inspection items and do the inspection. Just like you did at your house during the partnered inspection exercise.

10. The four-point inspection items to remember:
    - Roof
    - Electric
    - A/C
    - Plumbing

    Try to have the utilities turned on by the seller.

These are the expensive areas to fix, plus it affects the insurance you can have placed on the house. Make sure these four items are in good shape. Otherwise, you will need to factor the repair into your evaluation.

Having the utilities turned on by the Seller is helpful in the following ways:

- Roof: check for water spots in the ceiling; look for missing shingles, etc.

- Electric: you'll know that power is available and can check outlets and light fixtures. Look at the breaker box—the big switch at the top should be 100 amps or above; if you see 200 amps, it's most likely upgraded.

- A/C: you'll know that it works. For cooling and heating systems, aluminum wiring is *bad*; it starts fires.

- Plumbing can be checked for clogs, leaks, and water pressure. We want PVC, the white plastic pipes.

AGAIN, these are the BIG ticket items to be aware of!

These items, if there are major problems, can keep you from getting insurance, or lock you into expensive insurance.

If the property is occupied by a tenant, ask them how much they pay for rent, and ask about any problems or work orders they would like you to write up for them.

Final Step
End of Inspection

If the agent or seller has the contract with them at this inspection time, take it back to your "Partner" to sign and let them know you will fax it over and drop off the deposit (if applicable). After you get home, if you decide that you are going through with the contract, let them know you will send it over shortly. If you are no longer interested in the house, look over your numbers, re-evaluate, and then contact the other party with your decision.

There is a chance during the inspection that you may get turned off, but once you re-evaluate the numbers you may see that profits are still there and the repair items are worth handling—plus, you can always request that the seller fix those items which turned you off during the inspection.

Please do not make your due diligence period less than 15 days and the closing no shorter than 30 days. *Period.* This is adequate timing to accomplish the things you need to complete prior to closing the deal.

When you have worked out the details of the contract, both you and the seller have signed the contract, and the deposit money has changed hands, you have locked up the deal. **CONGRATULATIONS!**

Additional Notes & Review

Four-Point Inspection

Roof: check for water spots, missing shingles, trim rot, and rotten edges; if metal roof make sure it's good.
You might need to paint or seal it.

Electric: look to see if the power is on, check outlets and breakers; if main breaker box has 100amp service and above anything less may need an upgrade. 200amp is best!

A/C: look for outside A/C unit and inside air handler. Normally it's in a closet. Look for water stains around the floor—the drain line could be clogged, or the pan rusted through. Check the filter and see if the coils are dirty.

Look at the coils and make sure that there is no paint on them. When painting the interior of a house, painters at times turn on the A/C. If they used a sprayer, the paint floating in the air could have gotten sucked into the coils, especially if no filter was in place.

Look for aluminum wiring in, on, or around A/C units; this can lead to fires inside the air handler.

Plumbing: check to see if the house has PVC pipes (which are newer) or galvanized pipes (older).

If property is occupied ask the tenant if there are any problems or concerns, and write up a work order at that time for the issue.

At the end of the inspection, tell the agent you want to take the contract with you to have your partner sign it (this is a ploy to buy time) and work up numbers concerning anything the property is lacking. After this you have locked up the deal.

Some Questions

1.   If we do have to do any of these four-point inspection repairs, do we negotiate a lower price?

Once it's under contract you still have a 15-day inspection period. It's possible that the seller is now emotionally attached to the contract or the sale, so you can say, "I did my due diligence on the property and there have been XYZ issues. Would you please send me the receipt for the last repair you did on these items?"

If they cannot provide them, then you can either ask for credits at the closing table or have the seller fix the issue prior to closing.

If you requested for credits towards closing costs or requested certain items to be fixed and the seller said 'no,' that can be a deal breaker. This decision is dependant on you to negotiate. You know what you're comfortable with and you know the two criteria you *must* meet. You can negotiate something else whether it be less money down or additional terms to make your goal complete.

    a. If you're doing 10-CAP properties with the profit margins in place, you likely have money for repairs and still profit off the property.

If you choose to fix it with money out of your pocket, you can do a cash-out refinance. This allows you to get your repair money back.

MISTAKE: It's going to be hard to resist, but do not, *do not,* DO NOT, **DO NOT**, *DO NOT* take money out of your rental property to the point that it will affect meeting the two criteria. You will have created an *alligator*—we call it that because it bites your wallet every month.

Your property still has to cash flow properly, so do not get into negative cashflow. Hobby Millionaires *don't* invest that way.

b. Money goes down when the contract is signed, it is figured as part of the closing costs. The down payment is then be credited back to you at closing. Make sure this is stated in the contract.

c. Additional Clause to add to contracts: "Purchase price of the property to be the sales price or the appraised value, whichever is less."

This makes sure you don't spend money on an appraisal, survey, etc. and then not be able to purchase the property. The seller or agent should have a good idea if it will come in at the right number or not. They might even have an appraisal for you to use. If they don't like this clause, negotiate for them to pay for the appraisal if it does not come in at the purchase price. This way you won't lose money and the seller can have the appraisal to use later.

STEP #4

BUY IT!

What to Expect?

Training #4
Your Status

You're now under contract.

- You have at least 15 days to look over your deal in detail.

- You also have at least 30 days to close the property.

- Your contract states that your deposit is to be credited back to you at closing.

- Your contract also states: "Purchase price is the sale price or the appraised value whichever is less" or you have an agreement with the seller to pay for the appraisal if it does not appraise to the value the seller wants.

- This is where the fun begins. You will now learn the art of "Professional Babysitting." *Professional Babysitting is a must here!*

Buying the Property

REMINDER: To close with banks, you normally need the following. You will be pulling these items together to get to the closing table:

- Appraisal
- Survey
- Insurance
- Your financial packet (two years' tax returns, financial statement 1003, pay stubs, credit score)

Now think about the different ways to buy the property:

- Single owner: you only

- Joint Venture: this is when you purchase the rental property with other people. If you do this, the partner you have chosen has to be *needed* for some aspect of the deal—they could be a cash partner or a sweat equity partner where they do all the labor. Either way, they must bring something to the table. Make sure you both have the same goals in mind. You do this by using or creating an Operating Agreement. This explains who does what and also how to exit the partnership.

Network at your real estate clubs and private business clubs to find like-minded investors, and join the ones that worked for me!

Tips

- I suggest opening an LLC for each property (to hold title) and another LLC to manage the properties. If you don't, make sure to get properly insured with fire, dwelling, and liability coverage.

- Recertify an old survey. Find out who did it when the seller bought the property and get them to recertify it. This can save time and money.

- Use the prior title company. This, also, can save you time and money.

- Title insurance: makes sure the sale is good with a marketable title, no other owners, no liens, and no encumbrances.

- During this time—while you're pulling all of the closing items together—start marketing the property by placing signs at the nearest intersections and send people over to look in the windows.

- LLC with Partners: get everything in writing so you're all on the same goal path.

You make sure *everyone* is getting the items for the closing pulled together. You should contact them on the day they said something will be finished.

Professional Babysitting

1. If the survey is to be complete on Tuesday, then you make sure that the closing agent has the survey in hand by 4:00pm

2. If the appraisal is to be at the closing agent's office on Wednesday, check at 4:00pm to be sure the closing agent received it.

3. When insurance to be place, make sure it is.

4. Be sure the bank or funding players have all they need to get closing paperwork to the closing agent.

5. Then, make sure the closing agent has the HUD statement ready for your review.

Closing

Closing is the signing-of-the-paperwork party. It is when, and where, the transfer of ownership and title occurs. Having closing at the title company or attorney's office is strongly suggested. Yes, there are ways to transfer property in non-formal ways. I do not teach that. Hobby Millionaires are conservative and do things *right!*

Once the transaction is "closed," you or your legal ownership entity, has become the new owner of the property.

Remember to get the keys!

Additional Notes & Review

The Closing

When you're dealing with the bank:

1. Survey: get the seller to give you an old survey (this can save time and money); go back to old survey company, get it recertified, and you're done.

2. Appraisal: before you send out an appraiser make sure the bank approves of that particular appraiser; many banks are picky about the appraisers they use. Also, ask the seller if they have a recent appraisal.

3. Insurance: call around and get multiple quotes; every insurance company has their own rates. Make sure the policy is for at least the price you bought the property for (that way you're at least covered for your losses).

    a.   Fire dwelling insurance

    b.   Liability Insurance

4. Financial Packet: last two years' worth of tax returns (have them easily accessible), list of assets/expenses in financial statement, pay stubs, and credit score.

How you want to buy the property

By yourself or through a Joint Venture: a lot of times you can get further faster this way, and you have someone to lean on throughout the process—plus, you can motivate each other. Two heads are better than one.

Tips

- Buy the property through an LLC(the partners are the guarantors of the property).

- Open another LLC to manage the property (this LLC is also the public name that is displayed and plastered about with marketing). This LLC has no ownership, which provides additional coverage. If the management LLC damages something or causes a problem, then it doesn't own anything, nor does it have any money.

  Be sure to structure the LLC as a pass-through for taxing purposes. If you have other members in your LLC, you will be issued a K-1 at the end of the year. When you have an LLC, it covers you from the top down, but it does not shelter you from the bottom up. This means that you and your assets are protected if something were to happen to a property owned by the LLC, but if you were to do something personally, you open the assets of the LLC to being vulnerable—so please don't go running over small children or anything of the sorts.

- Get old surveys recertified.

- Title Companies: try to use the same title company that was used originally on the property. It can save you money by staying in-house. Title insurance can save you money in case there is a problem down the road with the ownership of the property. Title insurance is in place to ensure that the title was clear when you purchased it.

- Once you start negotiations on the property place a rental sign in front of the property or at the nearest intersection. This will allow you to start collecting leads of renters. The responses to this ad will also help you gauge what people in that area are looking for (i.e. 2 BR 2BA or 3 BR for $800/month, etc.) this helps you identify other properties or investments to look for in that area.

- Professional Babysitting: throughout the process you will be babysitting people to get your goals met.

STEP #5

Managing
Your Buy-&-Hold

Don't be a landlord

What is a "HOME GUARDIAN"?

"Time is valuable. Teams are best. Use them both wisely, and I will show you success!"

- Bonnie Laslo

Training #5
Your Status

Your legal ownership entity owns and controls the property or you own it yourself with great insurance, right?

Now for a reminder:

- You are *NOT* a Landlord.

- You are *NOT* a Property Manager.

- You are *NOT* an Investor with houses for rent.

You are a Home Guardian
on a team of Home Guardians.

Your Mission: to teach and train your team and your tenants.

Look at it this way and be open for the next two minutes. All your houses are babies and the tenants are the babysitters. If, they call you in the middle of the night, something is really wrong with your baby.

For a million dollars, will you answer a late-night phone call once every four months, if that?!

Would you rather rent from a Landlord, a Property Manager or...a Home Guardian?

Home Guardians leave tenants and property in better shape than before both came into contact with you. You have to understand that you *directly* affect the lives of the families and people who live in your rental properties. They are the ones who are going to set you financially free to live the life you wish to live!

Be Aware. Tenants are now playing on your team. You determine how well they play your game of real estate.

- If you think you'll have bad tenants, then you will.

- If you don't like tenants, then you won't have any.

- If you hate managing properties, then find someone who does.

- If you don't like people, then most likely a lot of them don't like you.

What you focus on expands and you will live the story you're telling yourself about taking care of your rental properties.

You can get the right people in place to get over this challenge, but I say that you're missing out on many *before* and *after* transformations that can give you self satisfaction—missing out on knowing that *you* were the cause of your own challenges and being able to watch the effects and the results unfold before your eyes.

People go to work and have a hard life as a renter. They are in the position of *having* to rent and would love to have a home of their own, but they don't for some reason.

Now they are under your care as a Home Guardian.

Allow them the peace and quiet of coming home to a place that's comfortable after a day of working hard.

Allow them a place to raise their families safely. Be there to guide them if they ask questions.

Even better, place them in contact with people who can help them if they are seekers. Seekers are people seeking for a way to improve.

I'm not saying to become each tenant's personal mentor, but any little thing you can do, do it. Choose to put it in play for them.

If you play the real estate buy-and-hold game this way, guess what? Approximately 100% occupancy and a world of gratification and fulfillment is the result.

How do I know this?

I know this because I run my real estate business this way. You can have the same results if you approach buy-and-hold real estate management this way.

I hope you get this. If not, as you move forward with the buying of rental properties, give it a whirl here and there and see what happens.

People have been wrongly influenced to think that looking over properties is such an 'awful' thing. If you can erase that from your head or create more experiences to wash away your bad prior ones, then you will see your results and wealth soar to Millionaire status quickly.

It will become easy for you, but at this point take as much of this mind et as you can and complete your goal of obtaining five properties or units a year!

Buy & Hold Management

Now that you own the rental properties: *Whooo-Hoooo!*

One rental property in the portfolio and four more to go!

This is where you CELEBRATE!

Go out with friends and family, and tell everyone what you did. You just increased your yearly income by $2,400 a year.

Just think if you had 10 of them, your 'hobby' would bring you in an extra $24,000 a year!

*Hmmm.....*Plus maybe $240,000 to $500,000 in net worth at that point. Plus, if you had 10 houses worth about $100,000 each, you'd have a million dollars in Real Estate Holdings! **Now that's GOOD Stuff!**

After celebrating,
come back to finish the set-up

You'll need a New-Management Letter if the property is already occupied by tenants.

Mock-ups (or 'staging') will be needed for property leasing if it is not yet occupied.

Tip: Borrow staging items from your own house.

- Sign with flyers in the front yard
- Wreath on front door
- Small table or end tables
- Couple of artificial plants in corners of rooms
- Kitchen and bath towels in place
- Curtains (if available)
- Lease application forms on the kitchen counter or on a table by front door
- Dish strainer with dishes
- Bath mat and kitchen mat
- Shower curtain
- Air Fresheners

Showings and Leasing

You want to avoid using the words 'small' (say "large room" and "regular-sized room" instead) and 'unit' (say "house" or "home" vs. two-bedroom unit).

Sometimes it's confusing to remember leasing vocabulary vs. investor vocabulary. Time and experience will solve that challenge for you.

It's better to meet your prospects and show the house to them, but you can place a combination lock (from any hardware store) on the front door and do showings over the phone, if necessary. I call this process remote management or off-site showings.

Tips if the property is not move-in-ready yet

1. If the property is still messy or not really ready for showing, tell the prospects they are more than welcome to take a peek, but the workers are still working on getting the place ready for them.

   NOTE: Drop off brooms, mops, tools, boxes, etc. for appearances. Showing *something* is better than nothing; otherwise, they might not come back.

2. Properties sell themselves, so don't worry. It's either going to be the right floor plan and price for them or not—just let them see it.

Leasing Paperwork

You will get the following signed and collected:

1. Application and Fee

2. Community Codes

3. Lease Agreement

4. Deposit money, rent money, or both, whichever you decide to get. Many times it depends on the current showing condition of the property. Timing also plays a large part.

We lease on a first come, first served basis!

And one more time: *we lease on a come, first served basis!*

WE GET A SIGNED LEASE AND THE MONEY.

WE WAIT FOR NO ONE.

THERE ARE NO EXCEPTIONS. PERIOD. END OF STORY!

We only lease to people ready, willing, and able to take immediate action and who want to become our tenants.

Note

If their application comes back awful, you return the money and let them know the application was not approved. Then, tear up the paperwork.

Once you have the signed lease paperwork and collected the money, you have until the move-in date to get the property ready for them.

In some instances with new acquisitions, the new residents might be doing some of the work or cleaning instead of paying a full deposit. This is up to you and it will vary depending upon the situation.

Move-In

Today is Move-In day!

- The resident has agreed to meet you and pick up keys.

- If they have not paid rent, you collect it now in *cash* or *money order*. They can use checks later if you choose, but for move-in they pay cash or money order *ONLY!*

- The resident brings you a Utility Confirmation so you know they have utilities out of your name and are not using candles and a bonfire to save money.

- You issue them a Move-In Checklist sheet (available on the Hobby Millionaire website) to document the existing conditions. Also, it has an area for them to list maintenance requests.

Done
Move-in Complete

Everyone dreads that emergency phone call in the middle of the night. Please look at it again in the following way. I will also provide you some tips.

Your properties are your babies. Your residents are the baby sitters. If they call in the middle of the night, then something is *really* wrong with your baby.

Typically, the call would fall into either the Fire, Flood, or Blood category, and normally there's not much you can do other than hold their hand.

Tips for Those Challenging Occasions

Create an emergency magnet with phone numbers for your chosen providers and put it on the fridge (or use an answering service).

The magnet should say:

After Hour Emergency #'s

- Plumbing issues: please call 777-7777
  (call to get quotes from a few companies)

- Health and Fire: please call 911

- Lock-outs: please call 777-7777 (Locksmith)

You will need to speak with the plumbing company, answering service, and any other after-hours emergency company for the person to make sure they know who you are and which properties you own. You can also have them call or text you if there is a really big emergency.

Eviction

Check with your city on the proper procedure for evicting tenants. Most are somewhat similar:

- Three-day Notice to pay rent or give up possession. Then, you file if they don't pay up.
- Five-day summons.
- 24-hour Writ of Possession.

If you have a good relationship with your residents (and you will since you are a home guardian and they really like you), many times you can work things out before it gets to the eviction stage.

Tips

1. Ask the tenant what's wrong.

2. Ask if they can find a more affordable place and leave by the weekend with no eviction on their record.

3. Transfer them to a smaller property.

4. Offer some or all of their deposit back if they can be out by the weekend—they can use it on the new place.

5. If you have side work going on, put them to work. Keeping your money in your community, as well as with your resident family, is great for resident retention.

Resident Retention

Our office offers 15-30-minute workshops after-hours for our residents. Credit repair, how to buy a house, property management 101, how to become a travel agent, etc. Anything that you have knowledge on, offer it to your residents to help them. Use your success experiences to better the lives of everyone you know. Of course, let them know this is what worked for you and tell them to feel free to research it just to be sure it's right for them. Remember you can only speak and share about your experiences that have worked for you.

Credit repair is a popular, high-demand topic. People pay thousands of dollars when they can easily learn to do it themselves. Learn it. It can only make things better for you and your residents.

Remember your mission: "To teach and train your team and tenants!" It's a *big* Win-Win for all parties concerned.

Your residents are providing you with a great lifestyle and excellent wealth-building portfolio experience. Be grateful for them because they are the reasons you're a successful real estate investor. They are people who rely on you to take care of their homes and to keep them safe while under your watch.

Many people forget that happy, satisfied residents are perhaps the most important component in many successful real estate ventures. Their current circumstances have made renting the most viable option at this time and they have come into your life, thank goodness, as a person who is helping to pay off the mortgage and the bills to keep the property cash flowing in a positive manner.

If you like your tenants, then you will attract more and more of them.

Home Guardians improve properties *and people!*

Additional Notes & Review

Property Management & Leasing

You're about to own a property or you might have bought it already.

You are not a landlord, you are not a manager, you are a home guardian on a mission of home guarding (be in a different mindset than the average landlord. Why? In short, most suck!)

Step #1

Send a new-management letter, especially if the property is a multi-family one. You need to get everyone into the same routine:

- Where to send payment.
- Who to call about maintenance.
- Where the new office is located.
- Who to make rental payments out to, etc.

Step #2

Most of the time you will have one house that is empty or vacant. You will need to stage it or improve it a little.

- Make it look nice and big.
- Get your For Rent sign.
- Put a wreath on the front door so the house can be located easier.
- Have your flyers and applications ready.
- As you have already let people know from the inspection, the windows are still open.
- If you have any small tables, they are good to have for your mock up.
- Rob things from your own office or house.
- The property will normally rent in one to five showings.
- Artificial plants.
- Kitchen and bath towels.
- Curtains.
- Dish drainer with dishes.
- Bath mat.
- Shower curtain.
- Air fresheners.

Showing and Leasing

Showings are exactly what they suggest. People call set up a time and you show the property.

- Big difference between leasing vocabulary and investing vocabulary.

    o House and home vs. two bedroom unit.

    o Avoid using the words small and unit.

    o Instead of older use vintage or historic.

- Even if the house isn't ready, just show it anyway and let them know that you have cleaning or maintenance items inside. Sometimes go as far as placing a broom or boxes in the unit to make it look like it's being remodeled or work is taking place. This will give you more time to pull the property together.

- The properties show themselves, so don't worry about your showing tactics too much; just stay pleasant and positive. It will be the right price or floor plan for them, or it won't.

- Understand tenants will balance things more if they really like the landlord or home guardian.

- Put a 'spin' on vintage properties. Decide on a theme for each property (i.e. sunflower house, papaya house, daisy house).

  - All our houses have red doors to make sure people notice them.

  - The name seems to really work out.

  - We have noticed that tenants like to have a name for their house.

  - Naming a house makes maintenance easier. This is wonderful when you have a lot of properties.

Leasing Paperwork

When someone goes to look at a property, don't take anything from them in bits and pieces:
no partial money; no rental fee.

- You will have them sign the community codes.

- You will have them sign the lease and application.

- Then you collect the money.

Lease properties on a first-come, first-served basis.

- We don't hold a property for anyone.

- We lease to people who are excited to be one of our tenants.

- Don't promise anything to anyone; save your time and money.

What if their application comes back and they have a negative background check? Simply return their application and money, saying they failed the background check.

Move-in Stage

You have a lease; you know what day they will move in.

- They have agreed to meet you to pick up the keys.

- Make sure to college the first month's rent as either cash or money order (remember, you don't know them yet).

- Get the utility turn-on confirmation from them.

- Give them a move-in checklist:

  - This gives them a chance to list all things that are broken or in bad condition.

  - Ask them to mark all things with a star that are major or really important to them. This way you can address those items first.

A lot of people will take an apartment *unturned* (not cleaned and readied for the next tenant) since they are in a hurry to get into your rental property early. They know and understand that a full maintenance or cleaning has not happened yet.

Simply note on their lease that they were willing to take it unturned (as-is) and can submit repairs in the normal work-order call-in fashion.

- You can waive the deposit or fee if the tenant is willing to take it unturned (it's your choice).

- If they are willing to do it, then it's great, because they are stating that the property is up to their specifications. This is great, because they are less likely to come back and say maintenance wasn't done correctly.

Touchy Things

Everyone dreads the emergency phone call in the middle of the night.

- If someone calls, you should think of it as something is wrong with your baby and the residents are the baby sitters.

- The categories that a middle-of-the-night call would fall into are fire, flood, or blood.

- If there are any after-hour emergency calls, make sure the tenant has a number to call (only for an emergency). Then talk with the emergency contact to make sure they understand what your emergency list is.

- Health or Fire = call 911.

- Lockouts: if people get locked out give them numbers of at least three locksmiths.

- You can charge an after-hour service call fee if you choose (usually $50-$100) if you have to go out and provide a key. You know what your time is worth.

- *Suggestion:* have in writing a list of things that would be considered true emergencies.

Evictions

With the eviction process I want everyone to check with their individual city for the procedure.

If the tenant hasn't made their rental payment, I normally wait till the 5th of the month to post notices.

- If they pay on or before the first of the month, they qualify for a discounted rental payment.

- Then they have until the 3rd of the month to make the regular rent payment. It's normally $50-$100 more than the discounted rent option.

- Do understand that if someone does give a partial payment you will have to begin the notice process with them all over again. Obtain a final balance date of payment, so you can tell if they failed to keep their word and paid the balance due.

- Again, be sure to get a specific date of when to expect the second part of the payment.

- They have until the 5th before getting a late-rent notice.

- On the 5th of the month our three-day notices go out on door to any late payers (but try to call the tenant first).

- This legal notice gives them three business days to either pay the full rent due for the month or return possession (move out). This is the start of the eviction process.

- Now after the three days (or whatever it is in your county or town), if they have not paid, you move forward. At this point, you file the eviction publicly. We go to the Clerk of the Court for an eviction packet. Many cities will have the packets available to you, or you can hire an attorney to do it for you. I enjoyed doing it to learn the process for the first time. Yes, you will be a bit nervous, but I have found most people will help you through it if you ask.

  Clerks and others can't give you legal advice, but they can give you an opinion or give you an example or tell you what they have seen other people do successfully to complete the process.

- Have a copy of the lease with you in case you need it, as well as the three-day notice, if that's what you used.

- The court normally then sends out a five-day summons or something telling the tenant to appear or pay, or both.

- Depending on the city, they have five business days to pay the court or bring their balance current with the landlord.

- Most of the time in my experience, if you have gone this far to insist payment or possession, people tend to move out after the five-day notice.

- Check the property to make sure people took their things out of the property.

- Check for toiletries and bedding.

After the specified number of days, if the tenant has not paid or moved-out, then you normally have to do a "Writ of possession" that tells them something like, 'in 24 hours we are coming to move all belongings to the nearest public curbside and the locks will be changed.'

- You will then come by with a sheriff to change the locks and remove their things from the property.

Please note that before the eviction process gets this far, there are ways you can stop the process yourself.

- #1 Check to see what's wrong with the tenant and talk to them first. See if something can be worked out, depending on whether it's a temporary situation or a permanent one.

- #2 See if they can leave by the weekend, so they don't get an eviction on their record.

- Things happen and many times if you ask them what's wrong, you can possibly help or make the situation a win-win.

- You can also ask them if they want to transfer to a smaller or less expensive property, if the situation calls for it—maybe a one-bedroom would be better, if they're getting a divorce, for instance.

- You could also offer the deposit back if they leave before the weekend. That way they have money for their next place and you can get the next paying tenant into the property.

Oh-ya, Home Guardians have wait lists.

If it seems like this is a temporary issue and it's something that this tenant doesn't normally do, see if you have any side work they could do for you, or if you know of anyone who might be able to aid them in making additional money. This gives them a chance to make it right, so they don't think we toss people out when times get rough.

Home Guardian's *never* give money to tenants or swap anything for rent.

If work is performed (even if it is babysitting, tutoring, mowing the lawn, washing cars, or putting in play any skill they possess), you or the person you referred gets an invoice from the tenant and the tenant gets a check—even if it's made out to their landlord, utility company, or signed over. It's the habit that is important to teach. Otherwise, you will be setting a poor precedence.

That one action of showing a tenant how to create an invoice, and get paid for following the process has started many small businesses. Most do not realize the simplicity of starting an LLC or business of their own. This same process goes for small contractors or friends who are not tenants. Spreading knowledge with simple training puts things in play.

It's like going around pushing people gently—they start to look around at the possibilities. That's all you're trying to do is wake people up a little.

It's fantastic to watch when it sticks to someone.

Resident Retention

Our office offers small 15-30 minute workshops for our tenants:

- Anything you have knowledge in, offer it to your tenants. Send them a letter letting them know.

- Credit repair.

- Buying your first home.

- Property management 101.

- Skills they can learn.

Your mission is to teach and train your tenants. This will create a loyal following of people that will be lining up to stay in your property.

If you want to learn it all and get into true property management, then that is when you can make big money. There will always be people with money who want to invest in real estate but don't want to do the property management side of the business. You can easily make six figures doing property management as a Home Guardian.

- Take care of the property and take care of the people.

- Notice that your tenants are taking care of your property when they call in a work order. Otherwise, you never would have known about the leak that could have rotted out an entire cabinet.

- If you take a positive standpoint through an eviction process, then chances are you're not going to walk into an empty house that's missing a refrigerator or has rotten chicken sitting in the living room.

- Nothing good comes from being a crappy landlord, but as a Home Guardian you have tenants who like you.

Come holiday time, you have Christmas cards with rent checks in them! They make and bring cookies, gifts and homemade goodies to you and your family.

This is because they are also your friends to a degree, because Hobby Millionaires acting as Home Guardian are fun and compassionate while making a ton of money being *happy!*

Property Management 101

Brief Workshop
Look up and Explain

* **Marketing for Renters**

    o Use For Rent Signs in yard & Ads in paper

    o Internet/Websites – craig's list, etc

* **Showings**

    o Occupied vs. Vacant

    o Models/Mock-ups. Make it look pretty!

* **Lease Signing**

    o Application, Lease, Community Codes

First come, first served; first come, first served, etc.

* **Move-In**

    o -Move-In Checklist

* **Maintenance**

  o Cosmetics vs. Codes

  o Seven days

* **Resident Retention**

  o Bag Holidays: Easter, Halloween, 4th of July, etc.

  o Join Us info: sometimes it's just nice to know it's there if they want it.

* **Evictions**

  o -Three-day Notice

  o -Seven-day Notice

  o -Five-day Summons

  o -24-hour Writ of Possession

Some thoughts from Bonnie's Journal Entries

Peek behind my curtains the day this book came out!

The Queen B...Hobby Millionaire and Home Guardian

So...it's ah, 3:27am and I recently woke up from a late nap a little while ago.

Just flew back into town:

...have a mountain of work (pulling 15-hour days by choice, since it's exciting at the moment and no time to sleep)

...a few businesses to work on (in all of which I have a piece of the pie!)

...social circles to run around in

...a gym to visit (an unknown place most of the time when I travel; my goal is to get better at that)

...and a puppy, actually a dog now, to rekindle with since I've been "Missing in Action" for the past month-and-a-half.

So......of course it's a perfect time to decide to get this book out of me!

Maybe it's just a way to make more room in my mind for some more good stuff or another business idea.

It's been a *great* day, I do have to admit.

My hope is for this book to be *blunt* for all!

Those people who are around me constantly accuse me of lacking tactfulness or being able to mildly sugarcoat things.

Plus, Bonnie-bonics. That's an inside joke for my friends reading this. For those of you who don't know me, I tend to make up words and sayings.

Little do people know, I'm probably just doing them a favor by directly giving them a layer of thicker skin for those tough people they will encounter in life.

Plus, instead of digesting all the "sugar", I'm spending valuable time getting to the point and keeping it *simple*......fast! Ha ha.

And making things happen!

#1 BAD IDEA for newbie investors: Hanging out with negative people

They will drain your energy and leave you feeling irritated. *Leeches* come to mind (as Sid and I have described it).

When you are around them, listen to every word and try to play devil's advocate. It's actually kind of fun.

You will run into successful negative people too, but chances are that something else in their life has made them turn to the dark side.

Avoid it as much as possible—only be around it when you have to (especially, if they are family members).

Good example: take it in like fuel for your car,,,and *run* faster toward success so you'll get away from complaining about whatever it is they're currently bitching about or saying can't be done.

But mostly I've experienced them talking bad about someone. They love to hang out, "riding that Gossip Train."

Here's something fun to do in those situations...practice throwing a positive spin on the conversation and just watch their reactions.

Examples of some favorite negative comments to look for and think of some positive spins for them:

1. Gosh, I work so much and I'm tired.

2. Nothing really new in my life, just same ol' same ol'.

3. He/she spends all the money we make and we just can't do anything.

4. I gave him/ her all my time and did this and that for them, and look how they treat me.

5. That person does none of the work, but people think they do.

6. They borrowed money from me and they never gave it back.

7. I wish I could _____, BUT _____,,, blah, blah, blah.

Y start thinking, I can't *not* hang out with this "negative person", because of "blah, blah, and blah". You begin thinking that you're trying to help them; they need me, they're my good friend, etc.

Wake up! This is an *excuse.* Why?

1. Misery loves company.

2. Being in the presence of someone more negative or messed up than you, makes you feel better about yourself. (Getting pissed at me? Well, just think about it; really, really think about this statement.)

3. You probably haven't stepped back from the situation and realized that you're trying to help someone who doesn't want to help themselves. Maybe they enjoy being miserable or the attention of having people listen to them. Sometimes it's like a train wreck or car accident where you *could* look away, but you just don't want to.

4. Just be honest with yourself and realize this is not a path to success or happiness and **get off that path**. Look for the yellow brick road or the fast track autobahn! It's more fun, plus you're moving forward vs. hanging out chit-chatting about negative crap with people going nowhere.

Don't hang out with "Sticks in the Mud."

Self crippling, I call it.

*Ask this question to yourself **out loud**:*

(*really*...clear your throat and ask this question, *out loud*)

<Your voice >

Why do I keep feeding myself toxic badness and expect to feel good and be mentally healthy enough handle success?

QUEEN B's BLUNT ANSWER:

You can't; it won't happen.

In short, people won't like you or trust you.

Plus, if you were too far gone being a negative person, then I can assure you, you would not be reading this right now.

Starting tomorrow, you will begin noticing who this "Negeoples" are in your life. Look at them, practice on them, and move on.

If you have kids, don't breed a "Negeople"; there already are too many in the world today.

DO-DO-DO
Hang out with POSITIVE people

Advice from the Queen B

This was the greatest day of my life in regards to change.

Positive people come in all forms. Pretty, not so pretty, small, big, male, female, poor, middle-of-the-road, and *rich!* So why not chose to surround yourself with *these* types of friends, etc., if you have a choice!

It's more fun! It feels better and they support you in whatever crazy, or logical, ideas you have, and everyone gets along.

Positive people also work things out and communicate (for the most part) on things that *matter.*

Things to do, people to see, how to improve things, how to help each other; bring to the surface why things are exciting and, for me in general, "I care" more.

In general, you will CARE...which MOTIVATES you!

Being around these types of people makes you think and see things differently. You will *think* differently.

Heck, at least now you're *thinking,* if you weren't already.

So, how can this change hurt you?

How can hanging out with positive people be a bad thing?

Surrounding yourself around good people is just a good thing!

I can't tell you how many times I have quoted, "Good things happen to good people."

Live and learn from that saying, because it worked for me and it has worked for every successful person I know.

People are attracted to you.

People like you.

You're a pleasure to be around.

Plus it has a side effect of "credibility" **especially when it comes to real estate investing and business.**

Toot your friend's horns and if they don't have any horns to toot, then you might want to invest in some new friends who do.

<u>CERTIFICATE</u>

TO A REAL ESTATE

HOBBY

MILLIONAIRE

EVENT

2 TICKETS

ONLINE REGISTRATION

<u>.HOBBYMILLIONAIRE.COM</u>

FOR MORE INFORMATION

BONNIE'S BIO

Bonnie Laslo

Born: Athens, Greece (Yes-o-yes, an Air Force brat).

Grew up in Little Rock, Arkansas...then Phoenix, Arizona...then Tampa, Florida...then somewhere in New Jersey (went to a high school there for 3 days)...then back to Tampa, Florida and finished high school...

(Who-hoo. Graduated #11 in my class, with a 4.5 GPA from extras from advanced classes which I had to sneak into during the 7th grade. Being an Air Force brat, my school records were not transferred, I guess, so I just told that school I was previously in advanced classes and they let me take them).

I went to the University of Florida in Gainesville...
(**Go, Gators!** Got a BS in PR. Isn't that the truth, but I do have to admit it has helped me in so many ways.)

Got into a family three-car pileup accident and I had a near-death experience. The accident broke my back, messed up my knees, my ankle was given a lovely plate with five screws, and a few forehead stitches to top it off.

There I set off on my mission and put it in play.

I had many obstacles to overcome as a child (a time in foster care, my best memories with the Henry's—they showed me what family means) and many challenges that fortunately did not take me out of the success game.

After searching for real estate information and educating myself in every way I could, I became financially free at the age of 23.

At 26, I hit my goal of having a million dollars in real estate...a year early. Thank you, thank you, thank you, Alex and Susan!

Between the ages of 28 and 31, I wrote my books and structured my multi-billion-dollar vision into motion. I have always lived by the principle 'good things come to good people.'

I'm living it today, and will for the rest of my life. I want *everyone* to do the same, because it all comes down to health, family, friends, and what you can do to leave your mark in this world.

What will be left by you, when you're no longer here?

I hope this book helps those who help themselves.

And I'll enjoy the ripple effects.

Real Estate...

Become an Investor

Home Study Course	On-Site Boot Camp	Joint Venture Teams

Program Includes

8 one-on-one Coaching Calls

Teleseminars

E-books

Joint Venture Opportunities

5 Boot Camp Sessions

5 Email Training Sessions

Access to over $50,000 in Training Materials

www.HobbyMillionaire.com

CPSIA information can be obtained
at www.ICGtesting.com
Printed in the USA
FFOW05n0234070616